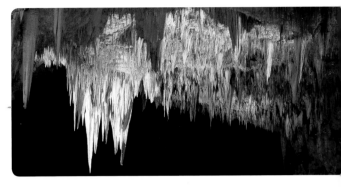

This book is dedicated to all who find Nature not an adversary to conquer and destroy, but a storehouse of infinite knowledge and experience linking man to all things past and present. They know conserving the natural environment is essential to our future well-being.

D1384528

CARLSBAD CAVERNS

THE STORY BEHIND THE SCENERY®

by Edward J. Greene

ED GREENE began his National Park Service career at Mammoth Cave National Park, Kentucky in 1966. After assignments at Wright Brothers National Monument, Cape Hatteras National Seashore, Bandelier National Monument and Big Bend National Park, he retired as the Chief of Interpretation at Carlsbad Caverns National Park.

Carlsbad Caverns National Park, located in southeastern New Mexico, was established as a National Park in 1930 and became a World Heritage Site in 1995. It preserves some of the best examples of limestone caves in the world.

Front cover: Crystal Spring Dome, photo by Peter Jones. Inside front cover: Entrance with blooming mescal bush, photo by Laurence Parent. Page l: The Big Room, photo by John P. George. Page 2/3: Temple of the Sun, Big Room, photo by Peter Jones.

Edited by Maryellen Connor • Book design by K. C. DenDooven.

Second Printing, 2007

CARLSBAD CAVERNS: THE STORY BEHIND THE SCENERY © 2006 KC PUBLICATIONS, INC.
"The Story Behind the Scenery"; the Eagle / Flag icon on Front Cover are registered in the U.S. Patent and Trademark Office.
LC 2006920234. ISBN 0-88714-265-6.

27

Colossal rooms filled with millions of cave formations, or speleothems, create a world of breathtaking beauty around every turn.

Billions of water droplets, each laden with a tiny load of calcite mineral, have built up the Temple of the Sun in the Big Room.

The Carlsbad Caverns Story

JOHN P. GEORGE

The story of Carlsbad Caverns National Park is actually the story of two parks: the one park visitors see on the surface and the one we see underground. The pitch-black underground is as different from the bright sun and blue sky of the surface world as the plants and animals of the Chihuahuan Desert are different from the rocks and minerals of the Cavern.

But, the two are also inexorably connected. What we see on the surface is more than the roof of the cavern; it is the very framework upon which the existence of the cave depends. Conditions on the surface continue to influence and impact—for good or ill—the subterranean world. But, it is Carlsbad Cavern, the underground world of stygian darkness, which has intrigued and beckoned visitors for over a century. Carlsbad Cavern is unlike any other cave on the planet.

It isn't the longest cave in the world; that honor goes to Mammoth Cave in Kentucky. It isn't the largest cave, or the deepest. What it is, is overwhelming. Nothing else in our experience prepares us for the combination of immense size; intricate, delicate shapes; and overpowering beauty that is Carlsbad Cavern.

Depending on the rate of water drips, mineral is either deposited on the ceiling forming icicle-like stalactites, or deposited on the floor building up stalagmites. If a stalagmite reaches to the ceiling, it is called a column.

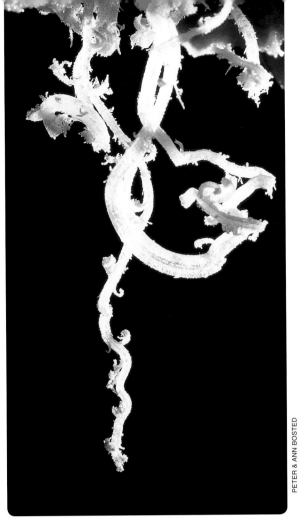

Carlsbad
Caverns
is Unlike
any other cave
on
This
Planet

Tiny crystals of calcium sulfate, or gypsum,
grow into intricate, extremely delicate shapes that
range from thin, hair-like threads to ribbons that
twist and turn reminiscent of baroque architecture.

The Capitan Reef
formed millions of
years ago along the
margin of an ancient
sea. Its rock layers are
the framework within
which the caves
of the Guadalupes
were formed. The up-
ward slope of the fore-
reef was instrumental
in moving hydrogen sulfide
water into the reef to
dissolve cave passages.

*What would one day be the part of
North America known as New Mexico
was then located near the equator,
and the climate was tropical.*

The Underground World

LAURENCE PARENT

The immense *size and overwhelming numbers of cave formations found in Carlsbad Cavern tell us that the climate on the surface here was once a very wet tropical rainforest, much different than the Chihuahuan Desert of today.*

PETER JONES

For only a few days a year *in late summer, the afternoon sun aligns perfectly with the natural cave entrance to form a brilliant shaft of light. Beyond the twilight zone, just inside the entrance, the natural condition of the cave is absolute, total darkness.*

The story of Carlsbad Caverns National Park begins more than 250 million years ago. As you would expect, the world was a much different place then. The plates that make up the earth's crust are constantly moving, sometimes imperceptibly, sometimes violently. By the beginning of what geologists call the Permian period, those plates had fused together into one giant land mass called Pangaea; a single super continent that stretched nearly from pole to pole. What would one day be the part of North America known as New Mexico was then located near the equator, and the climate was tropical.

Along the margins of Pangaea, fluctuations in sea level and tectonic action created changes in the shoreline, such as bays and lagoons, and even formed large, inland seas. One such sea, known as the Delaware Sea, covered much of what is now southeastern New Mexico and west Texas to a depth of about 1,800 feet. The view visitors see today looking south from the park visitor center and stretching to the horizon was the Delaware Basin, where the ancient sea covered the land.

Within the sea were varieties of algae and myriad marine animals such as sponges, marine snails, clams and other bivalves, fish, and even sharks. It was the sponges and algae that formed a shallow reef that began to grow along the shoreline. The clams, snails and other marine animals lived and grazed among the sponges and algae, in a living reef that grew just beneath the surface of the water. Over time, the sea level rose allowing the reef to grow taller as the living portion built upon the older, dead reef below.

The reef material that later cemented into rock, primarily limestone, is what is seen throughout the park today. Wave action pounded the reef and gravity caused portions of it, some the size of a house, to break loose and roll down the reef face into deeper water. This fore-reef would become instrumental in the later formation of the Cavern. Behind the reef there were shallow lagoons. Sediments were washed into the lagoons by streams, and layers of limestone were deposited during rises in sea level, forming bedded layers of limestone and siltstone now known as the back-reef. This reef-building process continued for millions of years, resulting in a sequence of rock over 1,800 feet thick, up to three miles wide, and extending in a horseshoe shape for more than 400 miles.

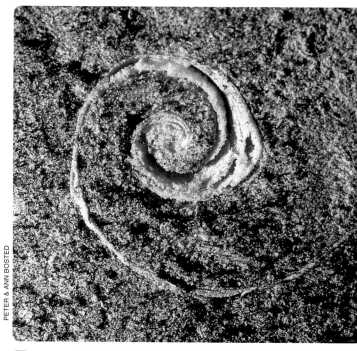

The Capitan Reef that forms the rock layers surrounding Carlsbad Cavern was formed by the deposition of marine life on an ancient sea floor. Although rare, fossils of the marine life may occasionally be seen.

Towards the end of the Permian period, the Delaware Sea was cut off from the main ocean to the extent that evaporation within the sea was taking place faster than the water could be replaced. Over the next several thousand years, the water evaporated, leaving gypsum and other minerals behind and completely filling the basin. For the next several million years, sediments continued to cover the area until the basin and reef were buried to a depth of several thousand feet. Still later, tectonic forces pushed the area of the basin and reef upward, and erosion carried away much of the sediment covering them, leaving the scene that visitors now see. Today, the Capitan Reef is exposed here as the Guadalupe Mountains, the Glass Mountains to the southeast, and the Apache Mountains to the south. It was these surface features, the Delaware Basin and the Guadalupe Mountains, that made possible the vast underground world below.

About 12 million years ago, caves began forming in the higher elevations of the Guadalupe Mountains. As uplifts continued, the water table retreated to lower levels; and around 6 million years ago

The ebb and flow of the ancient sea over millions of years formed the Capitan Reef as a series of rock layers. The reef, up to 1800 feet thick and 400 miles long, is mostly covered by sediment throughout its range, but is exposed at Carlsbad Caverns, Guadalupe Mountains National Park, and a few other places.

Carlsbad Cavern began forming. Most caves in the world are formed by carbonic acid. When rain and snow pick up carbon dioxide gas from decaying plant material, a weak carbonic acid solution is created. As the acid-laden water enters cracks and crevices in limestone and makes its way down to the water table, it dissolves the rock, and caves are created.

Carlsbad Cavern, and the more than three hundred other caves in the Guadalupe Mountains, were made in a different, much more dramatic fashion.

Deep beneath the nearby Permian Basin are vast deposits of oil and natural gas. Associated with the oil and gas is hydrogen sulfide, the gas that produces a "rotten egg" smell. As tectonic forces tilted the land and cracked the limestone, the hydrogen sulfide-rich water migrated upward, following faults and fractures in the rock and the slope of the rock created by the fore-reef millions of years earlier.

As the hydrogen sulfide-rich water came in contact with rainwater moving down through cracks in the limestone, it mixed with oxygen in the rainwater and created a strong sulfuric acid, nearly identical to the acid in your automobile battery.

This highly corrosive acid bath made short work of the limestone, rapidly dissolving it to form the huge chambers visitors see in Carlsbad Cavern today. Two clues that tell us about this cave-forming process are the steep slopes of some of the passages, showing us how the hydrogen sulfide migrated upward from below, and the preponderance of gypsum throughout the cave.

Carlsbad Cavern allows us to view the rock layers of the Capitan Reef from the inside. The process of sulfuric acid dissolution that formed these caves created the immense rooms and passages typical of Guadalupe caves. Some passages may extend for miles, while others are simply rooms that come to a dead end.

PETER JONES

Gypsum, easily dissolved by water, is not normally found in great quantities in most caves. But, in Carlsbad Cavern, you will see huge blocks of gypsum, up to fifteen feet thick in places. Gypsum is a by-product of the chemical reaction between sulfuric acid and limestone, and is perhaps the best evidence of the atypical cave-forming process that happened here.

But, the story doesn't end there. Within the past few years, scientists have discovered that caves in the Guadalupe Mountains contain life forms never imagined. Tiny microbes, single-celled organisms without a nucleus, have been found deep within these caves, far from any sources of light or food, the normal sources of energy for life. These microbes get energy by "eating", or metabolizing, minerals,

these Microbes get ENERGY by "eating", or *metabolizing* MINERALS

particularly sulfur, manganese, and iron. Evidence suggests that microbes may have accounted for the apparent efficiency of the cave-forming process by oxidizing hydrogen sulfide into the sulfuric acid that did the work. The huge caves in the Guadalupes may have been at least partially created by microscopic bacteria.

As the land continued to rise, and the water table dropped, chambers became filled with air and the cave-forming process ceased, only to continue at the new water table below. The Big Room was formed nearly two million years later than the upper level passages in the Cavern.

When the cave passages were filled with water, the water provided buoyancy and support for the rocks. As the water drained to lower levels, some of the rocks along walls and ceilings fell to the floor creating the rocks, or "breakdown", that you see along the trail. Since there is little weathering in the cave, barring the actions of humans, or an earthquake, rock fall is an extremely rare occurrence in the Cavern today.

DECORATING THE CAVE

About 500,000 years ago, climatic conditions on the surface were quite different than the desert environment we see today. Then, this area was a tropical rainforest. As the rainwater picked up carbon dioxide and followed tiny cracks in the limestone, it dissolved the rock. Each water droplet carried that tiny bit of calcium with it as it moved downward toward

Every stalactite and stalagmite in Carlsbad Cavern began as a single drop of water carrying a tiny amount of calcium carbonate mineral. As the water evaporates, it leaves the mineral behind and a speleothem is born. Since factors affecting the seepage and acidity of water are inconsistent, there is no way to calculate the growth rate of these formations, but the larger ones could easily be tens of thousands of years old.

Aragonite crystals have the same chemical composition as calcite ($CaCO_3$), but a different crystalline structure. Needle-like aragonite speleothems are not as common as calcite formations, but both are extremely fragile.

formation will be a thin, wide sheet known as a drapery.

Sometimes, water will be forced through pores in the rock under hydrostatic pressure and the resulting formation defies description. Called helictites, they might grow up, down, sideways, or in several directions at once, somewhat resembling roots, or Medusa's locks.

Under the right conditions, calcium will form crystals called aragonite. The Cavern's natural entrance serves as a cold trap, so there is a constant river of cold air flowing into the cave that you can feel as you enter the cavern. The colder air is drier, and as it moves along the cave passages, it evapo-

the water table. But, if the water entered an air-filled cave room or passage, the bit of mineral was left behind, either on the ceiling, along a wall, or on the floor. The result is the incredible variety and beauty of cave formations, or speleothems, we see in the cave today.

When a water droplet hangs on the ceiling long enough for the calcium to be deposited there, it will create an icicle-like formation known as a stalactite. If the droplet still contains some mineral as it falls to the floor, the calcium will build up a stalagmite. If a stalactite happens to grow over a stalagmite, the two may eventually join to form a column. If the water flows down a wall, it will leave the mineral behind to form a waterfall-shaped formation known as flowstone. If the wall is slightly sloped, the resulting

When calcite-laden water flows down a wall or across a floor, the mineral deposit left behind forms flowstone, a formation resembling a frozen waterfall.

rates the mineral-laden moisture from the rocks and formations, which leaves behind the mineral in the form of aragonite crystals. These crystals may be seen coating a wall, a stalactite or stalagmite, and are often called popcorn because they sometimes resemble that favorite snack.

Air currents in the cave can create another strange phenomenon. As the cold, dry air moves downward through the cave, evaporating water from the walls, it becomes warmer, rises to the ceiling, and becomes a river of warm, moist air flowing upward and out of the cave. When this rising, moist air encounters the cold, dry air entering the cave, it creates a nearly constant fog inside the Natural Entrance, just below Devil's Spring. When the warm, moist air comes in contact with speleothems, it dissolves some of the minerals, making them appear white and chalky. Since warm air rises, this chalky appearance will be on the top of formations, while new aragonite popcorn, formed by the cooler air, will form on the bottom. The Lion's Tail is a good place to observe this effect.

Since the climate here is no longer that of a rainforest, few of the speleothems in Carlsbad Cavern are still growing today. They are dormant, waiting for surface conditions to again change to a wetter climate when they will resume their growth.

The gypsum left behind by the reaction of sulfuric acid and limestone can also create a variety of speleothems. Since gypsum is an extremely fragile mineral, visitors must look closely and carefully to see intricate gypsum flowers, but are unlikely to observe delicate gypsum needles, long strands of gypsum "hair" or bushes of gypsum crystals.

Thousands of years of this activity by water and minerals has created a world foreign to our experiences in any other realm. It's a place where the mind forces the imagination to recognize familiar sights in the stone as a way of dealing with a totally unfamiliar world. Artful shapes become a Bashful Elephant here, an oversized Witch's Finger there, a Doll's Theater, or gnomes beside the trail. Each somehow provide comfort and convince us that this world is familiar, safe, comfortable. Huge underground chambers, massive formations—some as tall as an eight story building—all assault our senses and remind us that this world will never be totally familiar to us. Here we will always be visitors.

PETER JONES

Over time, calcite may seal cracks in the floor allowing dripping water to create pools, or even large lakes. Speleothems growing out of the pool, such as at Devil's Spring, started growing before the pool was formed, and will continue to grow as long as the water drips.

The underground world is so *unfamiliar that visitors often try to identify familiar objects in the myriad shapes and sizes of cave formations. Like viewing clouds, with a little imagination, one might see animals, gnomes or human forms in the rock. The hooded visage of the Clansman, located in Slaughter Canyon Cave, might appear frightening, but is merely an example of a large stalagmite covered by a thin layer of flowstone.*

Where water drips down a slanted wall, the calcite mineral will grow progressively further out from the wall as a thin edge. The result will be a thin ribbon, often appearing like bacon strips, or, given enough time, a broad drapery.

ARTFUL
shapes
become a
BASHFUL
elephant
or a
witches
finger

The names of several areas in the cave, such as Devil's Spring, Devil's Den, and the Witch's Finger, suggest that early explorers may have had some trepidation about descending into the dark, foreboding world below. With the addition of modern walking trails and electric lights, 21st century visitors need only find inspiration and enjoyment along the trail.

Some areas of the cave have been given more lighthearted names, such as the Chinese Theater. Here, stalagmites have the shape of characters wearing ancient Chinese costumes, as if presenting a play for the audience.

LAURENCE PARENT

Stalactites begin life as a tiny ring of mineral on the ceiling. As additional mineral is added, the ring becomes a hollow tube resembling a soda straw. Water continues down the center of the straw, which grows longer. Some soda straws in Carlsbad Cavern are more than ten feet long. If the soda straw clogs with mineral, water will flow down the outside, making it fatter and longer.

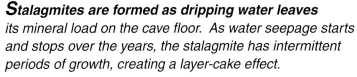

Stalagmites are formed as dripping water leaves its mineral load on the cave floor. As water seepage starts and stops over the years, the stalagmite has intermittent periods of growth, creating a layer-cake effect.

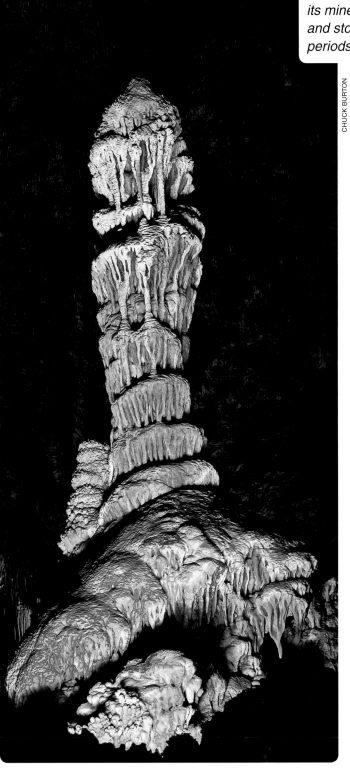

Just as early explorers, visitors today are greeted with new and unexpected sights around every turn. The Veiled Statue reveals a sense of the tremendous amounts of time and water necessary for its creation, as well as a grace and symmetry rarely matched in the man-made world.

In areas of high evaporation, water flowing down the side of a stalagmite will evaporate before reaching the floor, leaving behind a thin ledge of mineral. Over time, the mineral builds outward, away from the stalagmite, creating a bell canopy. The Mushroom, in Slaughter Canyon Cave, is an example of a bell canopy, with smaller bell canopies beneath.

As cold, dry air settles into the natural entrance, it creates a river of air flowing downward into the cave. This cool air causes popcorn to form on the lower portions of formations. As the air warms and picks up moisture, it rises to the ceiling and begins flowing out of the cave. This warm, moist air dissolves some of the mineral along the upper portions of existing formations, giving them a chalky white appearance.

*P*ools of water reflect a ceiling of white stalactites in Left Hand Tunnel. Visitors may take a Ranger-guided tour to this area where they will have a chance to experience the Cavern much as the early explorers did: in its natural state, without benefit of electric lights or improved trails.

PETER JONES

LAURENCE PARENT

*G*rand draperies extend from floor to ceiling in the Papoose Room, one of many exceptionally beautiful areas seen on the King's Palace tour. Even massive speleothems such as these are delicate and easily broken. The slightest touch leaves skin oil which permanently discolors the formations.

- 19 -

Lake of the Clouds is the deepest point in Carlsbad Cavern at 1037 feet underground. Huge, puffy, calcite "clouds", cover walls and ceilings. Clouds beneath the surface of the lake grew there before calcite sealed the floor creating the lake. Accessible only through unimproved passages, including a rope descent of about 230 feet, the area is not open to the public.

Calcium carbonate speleothems are naturally white, or even clear, but other minerals in the water droplets will give them added color. Manganese and iron oxide are common minerals that add color to the cave, but magnesium and even tannic acid from decaying vegetation can also affect hues.

Calcite-laden water, slowly flowing over the rock, creates the flowstone and ribbons of draperies that give a baleen-like appearance to the yawning Whale's Mouth. If deposited in a thin sheet, translucent calcite allows light to pass through, creating an effect that looks like strips of bacon.

CLINT FARLINGER

CHUCK BURTON

It takes little imagination to spot the Bashful Elephant, a group of stalagmites covered by flowstone. The underground world is a foreign environ-ment to most of us, and imposing familiar characteristics to the rocks, stalactites and stalagmites gives us a sense of belong-ing in this unfamiliar world.

Nearly everything here will grab you,
stab you, bite you, scratch you,
stick you, or make you itch.
But it isn't personal!

The Surface World

LAURENCE PARENT

The surface area above Carlsbad
Cavern is the Chihuahuan Desert,
one of four North American deserts. Far from being the parched, desolate land that
many visitors expect, the Chihuahuan Desert is teeming with several species of plant and
animal life, all specifically adapted for survival where water is in limited supply.

In spring, the Chihuahuan Desert comes alive in an explosion of colors as wildflowers vie for the attention of pollinating insects and hummingbirds. One of the most striking, the claret-cup cactus produces bright red blooms from April through June.

Artists' sunsets, steep-walled canyons, a hidden oasis, surreal plants like artwork from a Dr. Seuss book; the surface above Carlsbad Caverns is also a different world. At first view, the desert often seems stark, desolate, perhaps even foreboding. Nondescript limestone juts up from a blanket of tan and olive drab stretching as far as the eye can see.

Hidden beauty and complexity await those who look beyond the initial impression. Desolation is defied by deer browsing in the shade, a rock squirrel scurrying across the rocks, or a tarantula crossing the road. During the growing season flowering plants cover the desert floor with a carpet of yellow, purple, scarlet, pink and orange. Sudden storms can turn usually dry desert drainages into raging torrents, rushing water moving car-sized boulders like a child's toys. Seemingly unchanging, the desert is dynamic, abounding with a surprising diversity of life, but only revealing itself to those who seek to learn its secrets.

Carlsbad Caverns is located in the northern end of the Chihuahuan Desert, the largest of the four

Overleaf: The King's Palace is one of the most overpowering areas in Carlsbad Cavern. Photo by Laurence Parent.

Desert plants survive and thrive in an arid environment through a variety of adaptations. Lechuguilla, an indicator species for the Chihuahuan desert, has stiff, sharp pointed leaves that discourage browsing animals. The tight cluster of leaves provides shade for the plant's roots.

LAURENCE PARENT

North American deserts. Protected at Carlsbad Caverns and only a few other places in the United States, the Chihuahuan Desert covers 175,000 square miles, extending 1,200 miles from southern New Mexico, across far west Texas and deep into Mexico. From what we see inside Carlsbad Cavern, we know that this area hasn't always been a desert.

For the last 5,000 years, the region has been drying and becoming the desert we see today. One way to define a desert is a climate where the evaporation of water exceeds rainfall. That certainly fits the Chihuahuan Desert. The area around the Carlsbad Caverns visitor center receives an average of less than 15 inches of rain per year, most of it falling in the summer months of August and September. But that is an average; there can also be years of extended drought where only six inches of rain may fall.

Mountains to the west of the Chihuahuan Desert force warm, moist Pacific air to rise and cool. Since cool air holds less moisture, rainfall occurs on the western side of the mountains, leaving little water for the desert to the east. When the late-summer rains come off the Gulf of Mexico, they are monsoons, typical heavy afternoon thunderstorms that dump water rapidly, and sometimes violently, from the top of the reef to the plain below, cutting steep-walled canyons and creating flash floods.

While the desert may look desolate, it is teeming with an amazing diversity of plants and animals that call it home. Nearly 800 species of plants and more than 400 species of animals live here, many at the limits of their geographic distribution. And every one tells a story of specialized adaptation to this harsh, desert environment.

Nearly everything here will grab you, stab you, bite you, scratch you, stick you, or make you itch. But it isn't personal; it's all about survival in a place where water is hard to come by. Sharp points and jagged edges prevent grazing animals from devouring plants with a limited population. Cholla and the many other species of cactus produce leaves in the form of skinny needles that won't easily transpire precious water back into the air. Stems of the plants are succulent and absorb available water for long-term use. Some of the most common and easily recognized are several species of prickly pear that cover rocky ledges and areas of disturbed soil with their round, flat pads.

Also covered with thorns, ocotillo, which isn't a cactus, has a woody skeleton full of holes where water is stored during the rainy season. The spindly plant often appears dead, but it's merely waiting for the next rain, after which tiny green leaves will appear all along the stalk. In the spring, when sufficient moisture is available, ocotillo will be capped

Appearing dry, leafless, dead for much of the year, the ocotillo (o-co-TEE-yo) is actually dormant, awaiting the next rain. Then, the woody skeleton stores available water from the roots and soon tiny green leaves appear. In the spring, reddish-orange flowers light up the desert.

Scale-like leaves of the One-seed juniper transpire little water and roots are shaded by low, spreading branches. Blue, berry-like cones provide food for birds and animals, and at one time, even early humans.

with bright reddish-orange flowers that attract birds and insects.

Sotol, a member of the lily family, displays narrow, jagged-edged leaves that minimize transpiration. Clumps of leaves form the base of the plant and shade plant roots, also helping to conserve water. If spring rains come at the right time, thousands of sotol plants will each put up a single flowering stalk a dozen feet tall, making the hillsides appear like one giant porcupine.

Other water-conserving adaptations are seen in the creosote bush, a shrub that can live up to two years with no water at all. Leaves have a small surface area along with a waxy resin, both of which prevent water loss, and in times of drought the plant will shed leaves, and even branches, to make the most efficient use of stored water. The leaf resin also makes the plant mostly unpalatable for grazing animals, so the 70,000 square miles of creosote-covered landscape in the Southwest has no commercial grazing value.

Lechuguilla, a plant found only in the Chihuahuan Desert, stores water in succulent, very sharp-pointed leaves. It will put its energy into root and leaf production for several years before putting up a single flowering stalk up to sixteen feet tall, after which the plant dies.

Some desert plants, like this sotol, can grow into odd shapes, verifying for many visitors that the desert is, indeed, a strange world.

Though rare, springs throughout the Guadalupes create isolated areas of dense vegetation and serve as a magnet for hundreds of species of fauna. Rattlesnake Springs also serves as the domestic water supply for Carlsbad Caverns National Park.

Animals, too, use special techniques to survive in this harsh environment. Most spend the heat of day in underground burrows or shaded areas and only come out to feed in the cool of evening. Visitors may see any number of creatures, from mule deer to ringtails, snakes and javelinas, along the park road. Slow speed and extra care are always necessary.

One creature, the kangaroo rat, might be seen crossing a road, or scurrying through a parking lot. It is particularly well adapted to the desert and survives without water. It has the ability to convert water from its diet of dry seeds, and specialized kidneys dispose of waste without the output of water.

AN OASIS IN THE DESERT

In the desert one thing is certain: water is life. A well-kept secret at Carlsbad Caverns is Rattlesnake Springs, an oasis that provides the park's water supply and is home to hundreds of species of fauna. Birds, in particular, make good use of the dense vegetation and diverse habitats along the stream, and birders know Rattlesnake Springs as one of the premiere birding locations in the Southwest. Visitors can expect to see anything from wild turkeys to several species of neotropical songbirds, such as the summer tanager, vermilion flycatcher and painted bunting. Rattlesnake Springs is also home to dozens of species of dragonflies and damselflies, not a common sight in the desert. And, as the name indicates, visitors might even glimpse one of the three common species of rattlesnakes that inhabit the park. All wildlife in the park is protected, even the snakes.

Aerial Squadrons

At the natural entrance to Carlsbad Cavern, summer visitors are greeted by thousands of swooping, diving, spiraling cave swallows that nest just inside the entrance. They collect tiny bits of mud from area seeps and springs to form small half-cup nests on the cave walls. Common in Mexico, cave swallows have continued to extend their range northward over the last several years.

Cave swallows make up much of the day shift of insect eaters at the park. The park's most famous residents make up the night shift: the Mexican (or Brazilian) free-tailed bats. Each summer evening, hundreds of thousands of the small flying mammals swarm outward from the Cavern entrance to feed on insects along rivers, lakes and springs. They may fly up to 50 miles from their home in a single evening, and occasionally as high as 10,000 feet, as they forage on mosquitoes and moths. An individual bat can consume half its weight in insects each evening; a nursing female may eat more than its own weight in a night. The colony at Carlsbad Cavern will consume more than one million pounds of insects each season, many of which wreak havoc on cotton, corn and other crops grown in the area.

Park rangers present interpretive programs about bats before the flights, pointing out the benefits of bats to society and dispelling the common mythology that has grown up around the nocturnal creatures for centuries. Mexican free-tails spend their winters south of the border, but return to the park each spring and take up residence deep inside the cave, beyond the lights, noise and people. Here they raise their young, which are born in late spring and join the evening flight by mid-summer. Bats have been a part of the Carlsbad Cavern environment for a long time. Testing of bat guano has revealed that bats were in the Big Room 45,850 years ago.

Even though no one will be certain about
the first human to enter the cave, unquestionably
the man who brought it notoriety was Jim White.

Discovery & Exploration

The legendary discovery of Carlsbad Cavern is credited to Jim White, a young cowboy who stumbled upon the entrance around the turn of the last century. As the story goes, White was working as a cowhand for a local rancher. While riding the ridge looking for cattle, he saw what he thought was smoke rising in the distance. Further investigation revealed a cloud of bats emerging from a large cave entrance. Returning a few days later, he lowered himself into the cave on a homemade ladder, fashioned of wire and sticks, carrying only a lantern for illumination.

After the cave became famous, others claimed prior knowledge of it, but that would be years into the future. Certainly, American Indians had been aware of the opening. The first of these, Paleo-Indians, moved into the area around 10,000 years ago. The climate then was still much more temperate than today, with abundant savannah grassland lowlands and piñon-juniper forests in the mountains. The area supported populations of large mammals such as bison, mammoths, brush ox, and antelope, as well as smaller game animals, which Paleo-Indians hunted across the region.

Around 5,000 years ago, the climate here became more arid, not much different from what we see today. By then, the Paleo-Indians had been replaced by Archaic people, hunter-gatherers who survived on smaller game animals and plants, moving around the region in response to seasonal and long-term changes in the climate. These Archaic Indians used caves in the area, and it was probably they who first viewed Carlsbad Cavern, leaving evidence of their passage in the form of paintings on cave walls near the Cavern entrance.

NPS PHOTO

Cowboy, guano miner, explorer, ranger, Jim White devoted much of his life to searching out the mysteries of Carlsbad Caverns and sharing them with thousands of visitors.

Even though no one will ever be certain about the first human to enter the cave, unquestionably the man who brought it notoriety was Jim White. He spent most of the first half of the 20th century associated with the Cavern, first as a single-minded explorer, then as promoter, guide, and eventually the park's first chief ranger.

For thousands of years Native Americans crisscrossed the Chihuahuan desert following game and seasonal food supplies. Some discovered caves in the region, and fewer still left pictographs that told of their passage and activities. Some markings may reveal generations of messages about important life events, but their meanings are largely lost to us.

Early interest in the cave stemmed from a need for economic survival in southeastern New Mexico. When the cave was discovered to contain sizable deposits of bat guano, a local teamster named Abijah Long saw an opportunity. In 1903, he filed a mining claim on 20 acres surrounding the cave entrance and began a twenty-year process of mining guano from the Cavern. During the peak of the mining operation, as much as forty tons of guano were removed from the cave daily.

During this period, Jim White worked for the various companies that mined the guano, and

Deposits of bat guano, over 12 feet thick in Slaughter Canyon Cave, reveal that bats have used Guadalupe caves for hundreds of thousands of years.

Desert plants such as lechuguilla and sotol produce edible bulbs at the base of their leaves. Native Americans harvested these tubers and cooked them in shallow, rock-lined pits. Evidence of this centuries-long practice is seen across the desert in middens containing thousands of fire-cracked rocks.

continued his explorations during his "off" time. In the early days, no one believed the tales White told of the incredible underground display he was finding. That changed in 1916 after he convinced local photographer Ray V. Davis to accompany him into the cave to photograph the underground spectacle. Davis recognized opportunity and used his photos to begin an unabashed promotional campaign for the Cavern. He placed large photo-posters in hotel lobbies across the Southwest, printed thousands upon thousands of picture postcards, and even produced 100,000 windshield stickers, the forerunners of today's bumper stickers, that proclaimed "We visited Carlsbad Caverns". Soon people from around the region began visiting the cave, the beginnings of an unbroken stream of visitors that continues today.

As word of the unusual and beautiful underground chambers began to circulate, the federal government, in the form of the fledgling National Park Service, became interested in assessing what value, if any, it might hold. Robert Holley, a mineral examiner from the General Land Office, was sent to investigate the claims. Like so many before him, he was originally skeptical of all the reports of fabulous

Heavy machinery was sometimes hauled up near-vertical slopes to reach caves where it was used to extract thousands of tons of bat guano to be sold as fertilizer. Guano was mined in several Guadalupe caves during the early years of the 20th century.

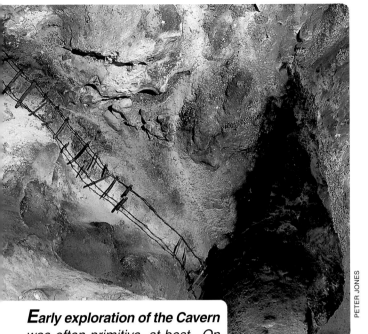

*E*arly exploration of the Cavern was often primitive, at best. On the 1924 Willis T. Lee- led expedition sponsored by the National Geographic Society, explorers descended 90 feet into Lower Cave on a ladder made of wire and scrub oak branches.

PETER JONES

size and beauty, but his final report probably summed up the feelings of most of those who have seen the cavern before or since. At the end of his April 1923 visit he wrote: "I am wholly conscious of the feebleness of my efforts to convey in words the deep conflicting emotions, the feelings of fear and awe, and the desire for an inspired understanding of the Divine Creator's work."

Based largely on Holley's recommendation for federal protection, on October 25, 1923 President Calvin Coolidge designated Carlsbad Cave National Monument. Within months, Dr. Willis T. Lee of the U.S. Geological Survey was investigating the Cavern and was inspired to publish details of his visit in the January 1924 issue of National Geographic magazine. Later that same year, National Geographic bankrolled Lee to conduct an extended expedition into the Cavern, and the resulting article and cover photo in the September 1925 National Geographic elevated the Cavern in the national consciousness. The public excitement generated by Lee's work stirred official interest in Washington, and on May 14, 1930, Congress designated the cave and surrounding land as Carlsbad Caverns National Park.

Cave Research

Research and exploration in the caves of Carlsbad Caverns National Park continues into the twenty-first century. The National Park Service depends on a cadre of dedicated scientists and committed volunteers to carry out projects ranging from survey and mapping of passages to documenting microbial life that may lead to the discovery of life on mars. Some investigators seek to learn more about the origin and age of

NPS PHOTOS BY SIMEON WARNER

caves, or changes in the cave environment over time, while others examine the impacts of humans and infrastructure on caves. Park managers rely on such science every day as they make decisions which balance cave use against long term protection of these fragile resources.

*A*s cave explorers and scientists push the boundaries of discovery, they continually monitor park caves watching for even subtle changes in the environment.

Participating in one of these tours will leave anyone with a genuine respect for the challenges of cave explorers, as well as the rewards of seeing amazing, unforgettable sights.

Enjoying Carlsbad Caverns

PETER JONES

Visitors can experience this underground wonderland on a number of different self-guided or ranger-guided tours. The Big Room is the star of Carlsbad Cavern. Covering an expanse of six acres with a ceiling up to 250 feet high, it is an improbable void in the reef, some 750 feet underground. Throughout, it is adorned with speleothems on the walls, ceilings and floors that simply overwhelm the senses. The Big Room route is self-guided, so visitors may enter the cave by elevator on their own schedule, and wander the one-mile trail at their leisure before exiting by elevator.

Also self-guided, the Natural Entrance route begins at the entrance where Jim White and other early explorers first entered the Cavern. The steep, one-mile trail descends to a depth of nearly 800 feet before reaching the Big Room. The trail is physically taxing, so anyone attempting the walk should be in good physical condition. After taking the Natural Entrance route, visitors may continue their walk around the Big Room, or exit the cave by elevator.

JOHN P. GEORGE

Speleothems come in a wide variety of shapes, sizes and even colors, depending on variables such as rate of water seepage, acidity of the water, mineral content and the surface upon which the water drips.

Cool air entering the cave often evaporates water seeping along the lower portion of speleothems. This leaves a tiny shelf of calcite as a base where newer drips add more mineral. The result: a stalagmite growing on a stalactite.

The flowstone-flocked Christmas Tree in Slaughter Canyon Cave sparkles with millions of tiny calcite crystals. Evaporation of water on the sides of the formation causes additional mineral to build outward in a bell canopy.

FRED HIRSCHMANN

The King's Palace is an especially beautiful portion of the Cavern that is available only by taking a ranger-guided tour. Beautiful, multicolored draperies, stalactites and helictites greet visitors around every corner on the 1 1/2-hour tour.

Other ranger-guided tours visit wild, unimproved sections of the Cavern, or other primitive caves in the park. Reservations are recommended for all ranger-guided tours. A visit to Slaughter Canyon Cave will give visitors a sense of what early cave explorers experienced before paved trails, electric lights and elevators were installed. Visitors will see remnants of early bat guano mining operations, as well as large, beautiful and unusual formations such as the Christmas Tree, and the hooded visage of the Clansman.

For the more adventurous, caving tours provide the chance to experience the cave on its own terms. Tours range in difficulty from walking along rough, packed-earth trails, to rock-climbing, crawling, and slithering along on your stomach through tight passages. Participating in one of these tours will leave anyone with a genuine respect for the challenges and physical requirements of cave explorers, as well as the rewards of seeing amazing, unforgettable sights.

TOURS *range in* DIFFICULTY from walking to ROCK climbing and *slithering* along *on* YOUR *stomach*

PETER JONES

PETER JONES

In Carlsbad Cavern,
*colossal rooms filled with
millions of speleothems
create a world of breath-
taking beauty around
every turn. On a guided
tour, Rangers lead visitors
into the King's Palace, a
crystalline ballroom where
time becomes a meaning-
less concept.*

The immense size of
*Carlsbad Caverns seems
to invite superlatives at every turn.
Such is the case with the stalactite
in Lower Cave known as the
Texas Toothpick.*

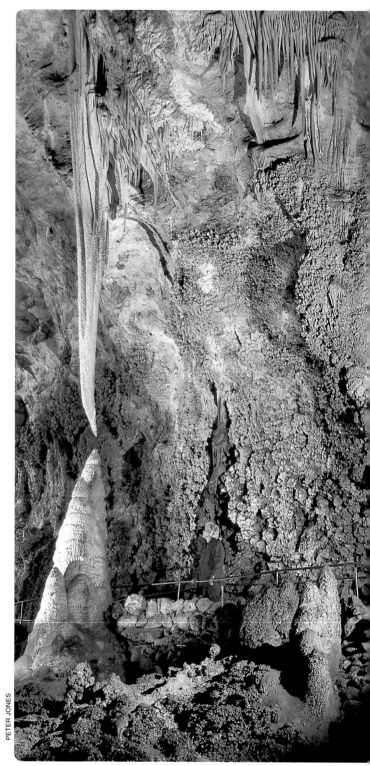

***T**he Sword of Damocles hangs precariously over all* who pass along the Big Room trail. But, there is little real threat; the sword, and the rest of the cave environment, is extremely stable.

***S**talagmites in the Big Room reveal a slow, drip* by drip deposition of microscopic calcite over thousands and thousands of years. Speleothems, some more than a million years old, are extremely fragile, and even the largest can be irreversibly damaged by the slightest touch.

PETER JONES

Careful observation into even the smallest grottos may reveal hidden wonders such as the Doll's Theater, a forest of tiny soda straws in the Big Room. To reach this part of the cave and create speleothems, water must percolate down from the surface to a depth of 750 feet, a journey that may take several months, or even years.

PETER JONES

The White Giant, a stalagmite of nearly pure calcite, can only be visited after an arduous crawl through small passageways and tight constrictions.

Lechuguilla Cave

The story continues today with continuing discoveries and new insights into the complexities of the park. Because of the way these caves are created, it is impossible to predict what passages may as yet be undiscovered or where a passage may lead. A huge chamber may abruptly end, or a miserable little crack in the rocks may lead to massive openings that extend for miles. The only way to know is to go. Cavers, those who explore caves, are a hale and hearty lot, willing to undergo privations, take on extreme conditions, and push their bodies beyond the normal limits of fatigue, usually with nothing more than a hope that they will find the new, the rare, the beautiful, the undiscovered.

The work of one such group in the mid-1980s was rewarded far beyond their greatest expectations. In consultation with the National Park Service, working in the bottom of a shallow pit, the group

PETER JONES

***C**aving isn't for the faint of heart. Fear of heights, claustrophobia, fear of the dark or fear of the unknown are all disqualifying.*

dug through rubble, following air blowing through fissures in the rocks (a sign cavers know that indicates bigger openings beyond). After several weekends of digging, the group broke through into one of the most significant cave discoveries of the 20th century: Lechuguilla Cave.

Located about four miles from Carlsbad Cavern, Lechuguilla Cave has no known connection with its more famous neighbor, but it has established its own reputation for the spectacular. Exploration since its discovery has shown Lechuguilla to be the deepest limestone cave in the United States at 1,621 feet deep, and more than 115 miles in length, with more passages found every year. Since it was unknown before 1986, the cave has enjoyed unprecedented care and protection by the caving community and the National Park Service. Only well-qualified cavers and research scientists are allowed to enter the cave on a few sanctioned exploration trips each year.

The reason for such stringent controls is that Lechuguilla Cave has revealed an unrivalled beauty, an intriguing assemblage of heretofore unseen microbial

PETER & ANN BOSTED

***O**nly recently discovered, Lechuguilla Cave is closed to all but research and exploration expeditions. Within its chambers are preserved crystal clear lakes, extremely rare speleothems, and as yet unnumbered species of microbes new to science.*

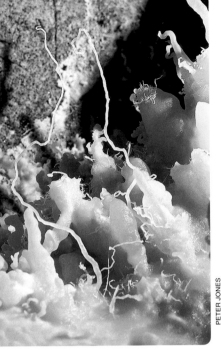

Helictites are calcite formations that grow in any direction, defying gravity, and sometimes belief.

PETER JONES

PETER & ANN BOSTED

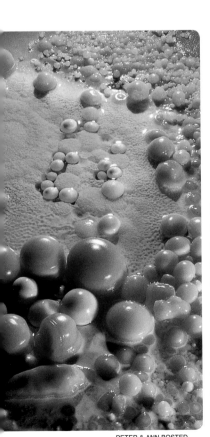

PETER & ANN BOSTED

Caves pearls are concretions found in cave pools, or where pools once existed. Mineral-laden water dripping into the pool loses carbon dioxide and precipitates calcite into the pool. When the calcite forms around the nucleus of a sand grain, the pearl is born. Additional calcite evenly attaches around the pearl, resulting in the spherical shape, although pearls may be cylindrical or elliptical. Additional calcite may cement pearls to the floor, or they may be found loose.

Some of the largest gypsum chandeliers in the world are found in Lechuguilla Cave. Gypsum is a natural byproduct of the chemical reaction between sulfuric acid and limestone, and hints at how Guadalupe caves were created. Some of these chandeliers approach 20 feet in length.

- 41 -

Precipitated calcite suspended in a pool may form rafts, floating on top of the water, or shelfstone, growing along the pool edge. Stalactites may grown down and attach to the shelfstone.

PETER & ANN BOSTED

PETER JONES

As supersaturated calcite water evaporates, calcite is precipitated as rounded crystals. As calcium is lost, elevated magnesium levels in the water then cause needle-like aragonite crystals to form instead of calcite.

The Red Seas region of Lechuguilla Cave is an example of calcite colored by iron impurities, capped by pure white aragonite crystals.

PETER & ANN BOSTED

The oddly pointed stalagmite found in Underground Atlanta in Lechuguilla Cave is the result of air moving through the cave. Warm, moist air will erode speleothems by absorbing minerals from their surface, giving them a chalky-white appearance.

A water drop adds its calcite to a soda straw on the end of an helictite.

life, and an unprecedented number and variety of exceptional speleothems, many of which are found no where else on earth. Some defy credulity, such as twenty-foot gypsum chandeliers, and equal-length gypsum hairs and beards. Some defy explanation, such as hydromagnesite balloons. Formation of these blisters or bubbles is poorly understood. Apparently, as moisture seeps from cave walls under pressure, it releases some of its carbon dioxide. Sometimes, the solution encounters a thin, paste-like film of carbonate minerals known as "moonmilk" on the wall. Hydromagnesite is the magnesium-rich variety of "moonmilk", so when the carbon dioxide pushes the "moonmilk" film outward, it forms a small hydromagnesite balloon, similar to a bubble-gum bubble. Such balloons are extremely rare, and perhaps a half dozen have been found in Lechuguilla Cave. Other speleothems are just impossible, like subaqueous helictites that grow underwater. Such are the secrets of caves, and the rewards that draw cavers and scientists ever deeper into the earth.

Carlsbad Caverns is a fascinating juxtaposition between the bright, often hot, seemingly stark Chihuahuan desert and the dark, cool, indescribable beauty of the caverns below. This fascination has drawn humans from Archaic Indians to 21st century visitors, each seeking a personal connection with these two, contrasting natural phenomena. For nearly a century, the National Park Service has worked diligently to facilitate visitor enjoyment and appreciation of these wonders, while at the same time, striving to preserve the often fragile, often unique, often irreplaceable resources for the next and future generations. While the desert has its own mysteries to explore, for tens of millions of visitors it is the underground world that is awe-inspiring. Nothing in our everyday existence prepares us to comprehend the vast amounts of time and water, the complex chemistry, and the sequence of geologic events necessary to create the overpowering size and beauty of the caves found in Carlsbad Caverns National Park.

The massive rooms typical of Guadalupe caves result from the aggressive dissolution of limestone by sulfuric acid. Most caves in the world are created by the less volatile action of carbonic acid.

All About Carlsbad Caverns National Park

The Carlsbad Caverns Guadalupe Mountains Association (CCGMA) is a private, non-profit organization whose main objectives are to provide interpretive materials for park visitors and to support the purposes and mission of the National Park Service at Carlsbad Caverns and Guadalupe Mountains National Parks, and the lands related to them in New Mexico and Texas. The goals of CCGMA are accomplished through educational programs utilizing a variety of media, and scientific investigations resulting in a greater appreciation of those resources being conserved.

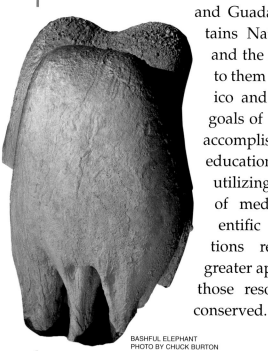

BASHFUL ELEPHANT
PHOTO BY CHUCK BURTON

Junior Ranger

To become a Junior Ranger, children age 4-13 complete a booklet of activities about Carlsbad Caverns National Park. Upon completion of the booklet, you will be awarded a certificate and patch. Wear it with pride!

This book is dedicated to the memory of Jack White Jr. He was the owner of "White's City" and was a much admired local legend in the business community.

Contact Us

Carlsbad Caverns National Park
3225 National Parks Highway
Carlsbad, NM 88220

By Phone
Visitor Information
(505) 785-2232

By fax
(505) 785-2302

Website
www.nps.gov/cave

THE WORLD RECOGNIZES CARLSBAD CAVERN

Due in large measure to the unsurpassed values of Lechuguilla Cave, as well as the world-class resources of Carlsbad Cavern, on December 6, 1995, Carlsbad Caverns National Park was designated a World Heritage Site by the United Nations World Heritage Centre. The designation adds Carlsbad Caverns to an impressive list of cultural sites and natural landscapes from around the world, including the Great Wall of China; Galapagos National Park, Ecuador; Serengeti National Park, Tanzania; and the Pyramid Fields of Egypt. Each of these sites are considered to have such unique international value that they should be considered a world heritage trust for people the world over.

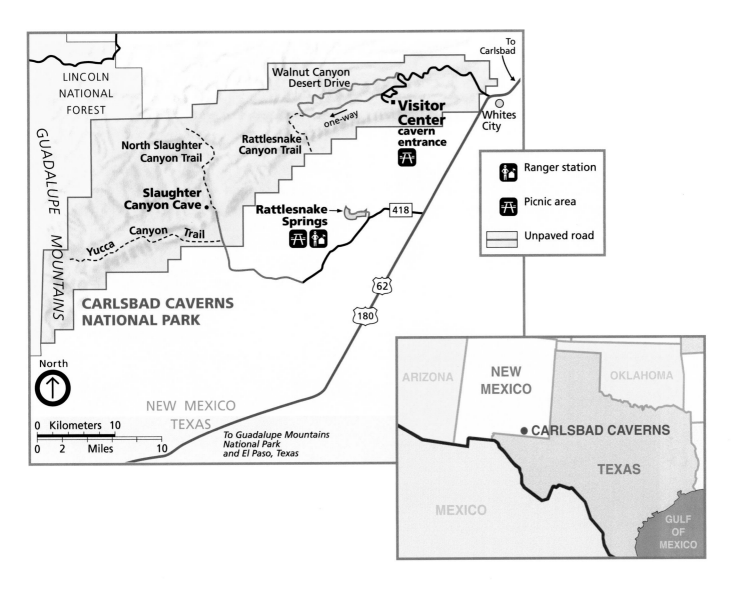

Enjoying the Surface World

While caves are the primary focus of the park, opportunities also exist for visitors to enjoy the Chihuahuan Desert atop the Caverns. A good place to begin is along the 9-mile Desert Loop Drive that begins near the visitor center and ends farther down the main park road. It provides a good overview of the desert and lets you get close enough to examine plants in detail. The road is open during daylight hours.

In addition to the summer evening Bat Flight programs, rangers often provide guided hikes along desert trails exploring the flora and fauna that call the Chihuahuan Desert home. Birders know Rattlesnake Springs as a premier birding site in the Southwest, so check at the visitor center for birding information.

Since the desert can be uncomfortably hot, cold, or windy, rangers offer a variety of slide programs, talks and demonstrations in the visitor center nearly every day.

Suggested Readings

BAKER, JAMES K. *What About Bats?* Carlsbad Caverns Natural History Association, 1961.

BURNHAM, BRAD. *Carlsbad Caverns: America's Largest Underground Chamber.* New York: Rosen Publishing Group, 2003.

NYMEYER, ROBERT. *Carlsbad, Caves, and a Camera.* Carlsbad Caverns Natural History Association, 1993.

NYMEYER, ROBERT AND HALLIDAY, WILLIAM R. *Carlsbad Caverns The Early Years.* Carlsbad Caverns Natural History Association, 1991.

SCHNEIDER, BILL. *Hiking Carlsbad Caverns & Guadalupe Mountains National Parks.* California: Falcon, 2005.

WIDMER, URS. *Lechuguilla - Jewel of the Underground.* Switzerland: Speleo Projects, 1998.

WHITE, JAMES LARKIN. *Jim White's Own Story.* 1932 republished by Carlsbad Caverns Natural History Association, 1998.

Suggested Web Sites

www.caves.org
www.batcon.org
www.batconservation.org
www.cavebooks.com

Looking to the Future

The result of unimaginable amounts of time and water, the caves of Carlsbad Caverns National Park are at once transcendent and temporal. Caves, perhaps more than any other natural resource, are impacted by the mere presence of people. Unlike the surface world, within the cave environment there is very little weathering to wear away graffiti, or soften the sharp edges of a broken formation. Million-year-old life forms killed by the introduction of a foreign substance into a cave pool will never be replaced. Careless actions of some visitors a century ago still resonate as if they happened only yesterday.

Still, we find it imperative that we visit caves, to see for ourselves. Perhaps it's a subconscious connection with our ancestors who once found shelter in caves, or perhaps a humbling realization that there are still many things in our world that we don't understand, or that we haven't even discovered. But, as tens of millions of visitors will attest, Carlsbad Caverns National Park touches us at our core, and presents to us one of the most awe-inspiring and memorable spectacles in all creation.

LAURENCE PARENT

Centuries of erosion have exposed layers of the Capitan reef in deep, steep-walled canyons. Sudden summer thunderstorms can turn normally dry, desert canyons into raging torrents, sometimes moving car-sized boulders down stream.

KC Publications has been the leading publisher of colorful, interpretive books about National Park areas, public lands, Indian lands, and related subjects for over 43 years. We have 6 active series—over 125 titles—with Translation Packages in up to 8 languages for over half the areas we cover. Write, call, or visit our web site for our full-color catalog.

Our series are:

The Story Behind the Scenery® – Compelling stories of over 65 National Park areas and similar Public Land areas. Some with Translation Packages.

in pictures... The Continuing Story® – A companion, pictorially oriented, series on America's National Parks. All titles have Translation Packages.

For Young Adventurers® – Dedicated to young seekers and keepers of all things wild and sacred. Explore America's Heritage from A to Z.

Voyage of Discovery® – Exploration of the expansion of the western United States.

Indian Culture and the Southwest – All about Native Americans, past and present.

Calendars – For National Parks in dramatic full color, and a companion Color Your Own series, with crayons.

To receive our full-color catalog featuring over 125 titles—Books, Calendars, and other related specialty products:
Call (800-626-9673), fax (702-433-3420), write to the address below, or visit our web sites at www.kcpub.com and www.kcspeaks.com

Published by KC Publications, 3245 E. Patrick Ln., Suite A, Las Vegas, NV 89120.

Inside Back Cover:
Visitors leave daylight behind as they descend into Slaughter Canyon Cave. Photo by Peter & Ann Bosted

Back Cover:
The lure of the unknown draws explorers, scientists and visitors, each to their own discoveries. Photo by Chuck Burton

Created, Designed, and Published in the U.S.A.
Printed by Tien Wah Press (Pte.) Ltd, Singapore
Pre-Press by United Graphic Pte. Ltd